A ROOKIE READER

ANIMAL BABIES

By Bobbie Hamsa

Illustrations by Tom Dunnington

Prepared under the direction of Robert Hillerich, Ph.D.

CHILDREN'S PRESS
A Division of Grolier Publishing
Sherman Turnpike
Danbury, Connecticut 06816

Library of Congress Cataloging in Publication Data

Hamsa, Bobbie.
  Animal babies.

  (A Rookie Reader)
  Summary: Provides drawings and names of baby
animals, including a kitten, a fawn, a piglet, and a lamb.
  1. Animals—Infancy—Juvenile literature.
[1. Animals—Infancy] I. Dunnington, Tom, ill.
II. Title. III. Series.
QL763.H36   1985   599'.039   84-27459
ISBN 0-516-02066-8

✓ Ƶ ɾƖ 599.039 H

A baby cat is a kitten.

A baby dog is a pup.

A baby deer is a fawn

until he's all grown up.

A baby pig is a piglet.

9

A baby horse is a foal.

A baby cow is a calf

until she's one year old.

A baby owl is an owlet.

A baby fish is a fry.

A baby kangaroo is a joey
until he's three feet high.

A baby rabbit is a bunny.

19

A baby bird is a chick.

22

A baby sheep is a lamb.

A baby beaver is a kit.

A baby lion is a cub.

(A baby bear is, too.)

A baby goat is a kid

and so are you!

WORD LIST

a	cub	is	piglet
all	deer	joey	pup
and	dog	kangaroo	rabbit
are	fawn	kid	sheep
baby	feet	kit	she's
bear	fish	kitten	so
beaver	foal	lamb	three
bird	fry	lion	too
bunny	goat	old	until
calf	grown	one	up
cat	he's	owl	year
chick	high	owlet	you
cow	horse	pig	

About the Author

Bobbie Hamsa was born and raised in Nebraska and has a Bachelor of Arts Degree in English Literature. She is an advertising copywriter for Bozell & Jacobs, Inc., writing print, radio, and television copy for many accounts, including "Mutual of Omaha's Wild Kingdom," the five-time Emmy Award winning wild animal series. She is the author of the popular series of books called Far-Fetched Pets, also published by Childrens Press. Bobbie lives in Omaha with her husband, Dick Sullivan, and children, John, Tracy, and Kenton.

About the Artist

Tom Dunnington hails from the Midwest, having lived in Minnesota, Iowa, Illinois, and Indiana. He attended the John Herron Institute of Art in Indianapolis and the American Academy of Art and the Chicago Art Institute in Chicago. He has been an art instructor and illustrator for many years. In addition to illustrating books, Mr. Dunnington is working on a series of paintings of endangered birds (produced as limited edition prints). His current residence is in Oak Park, Illinois, where he works as a free-lance illustrator and is active in church and community youth work.